THE SOLE BALM

A Chaplain's Musings

By
Elmon Krupnik

aBM

Published by:
A Book's Mind
PO Box 272847
Fort Collins, CO 80527

Table of Contents

My Musings

While serving as the command chaplain at the Marine Corps Logistics Base (MCLB) in Barstow, California, I wrote articles for the base paper and the local newspaper. I have compiled these articles to remind us that God inspires us through everyday events. Through that inspiration, God provides us with the only balm that truly heals as we journey each day of our lives.

The intent of The Sole Balm is not to just share stories but, also, to create a catalyst for learning and growth in developing your personal identity. Therefore, each article is followed by a "My Musings" page with three headings: Light, Life, and Lead. Light – what has the article revealed to you? Life – how can you apply what you have learned? and Lead – how can you apply the principles you have learned to help others?

It is my prayerful hope that applying these articles to your life will assist you in discovering and developing your personal identity.

Blessings to all,
Chaplain Krupnik

Dedication

Without the support of my family, I would not be where I am today (nor would I have many of the everyday experiences to draw from that form the basis of this book). I would like to dedicate this book to my wife Lynn, my children, Jennifer, Elmon Jr., Timothy, and James, and their spouses, David, Brittany, Ashley, and Katy, and my grandchildren, Jonathan, Joshua, Eli, Noah, Addison, Elmon Graham, Emery, Jadon, Lilly, Matthew, Elizabeth, Riley, Lucy, and Benjamin.

Preface

Part of our routine self-care is using ointments, oils, salves and balms to heal physical ailments and to maintain our health. Daily we take stock of our physical wellbeing, doing what we need to for our bodies and being guided to do what is best for our health. So too, should we attend to our emotional, mental and spiritual health and wellbeing. To be truly healthy and whole, we must find the balance and harmony of these four dimensions of our human nature. What better way to see beyond our physical nature than taking note of the world around us and the events we experience, and then look inward and reflect. Elmon Krupnik provides an excellent source of such treatment of our wellbeing beyond our physical nature. I hope you find the opportunity to reflect on each of his glimpses of life's events and musings over the insight beyond the obvious and find deeper meaning and lessons. Reflection is truly a soothing balm from the Source that brings comfort in knowing there is purpose and meaning to our daily lives. May you be challenged and inspired, but more importantly encouraged to pursue true wholeness of mind, body and spirit and in doing so experience the true Joy of Life.

Colonel Mark A. Costa, USMC (ret.), Ph.D., USNA (73),
Healing Touch Certified Practitioner,

Chaplain Krupnik's former Commanding Officer

Foreword

The sole balm for the afflicted is to be alone in the presence of the sole Being, who can read the feelings and thoughts of our hearts truly and entirely, for faint and imperfect is our expression of them to our fellowmen. How much more intimate is the connexion between the soul and its Creator, than between the soul and any of its fellow creatures!

Not even the tenderest heart, and next our own,
Knows half the reasons why we smile and sigh.
Each in his hidden sphere of joy or woe
Our hermit spirits dwell, and range apart;
Our eyes see all around in gloom or glow-
Hues of their own, fresh borrowed from the heart.

Richard Bentley, Constancy and Contrition, London: Schulze & Co., 1844, p. 116.

About the Author

Elmon Krupnik married his wife, Lynn (now a practicing attorney) in 1981. They have four adult children and 14 grandchildren.

Professor Krupnik is an adjunct faculty member and instructs in the areas of history, philosophy, religion and military science at the undergraduate and graduate levels. He holds a Ph.D. in Education from Capella University, a M.Div. from Midwestern Baptist Theological Seminary, and a B.A. in History from the University of Minnesota. He also is Senior Service College Complete and graduated from the non-resident programs of the U.S. Air Force Air War College and Marine Corps and Army Command and General Staff Colleges.

Chaplain Krupnik serves as Chief of a Medical Center's Chaplain Service, Chairman of the Military Chaplain Commission for a religious denomination, and as a Senior Chaplain (with the rank of Colonel) in a reserve component of the U.S. Armed Forces.

LIGHT - MIND OF GOD

LIFE - MEMORY OF GOD

LEAD - MISSION OF GOD

Faith, Family, Football

On Friday evening, September 22, 2000, I went to the Barstow High School Aztec football game. I purchased a football program and noticed on the top of the first page the words, "Faith, Family, Football." I must admit the words "Faith" and "Family" caught me off guard at a high school football game. I began to think about the words and the relationship they have with each other.

A good description of faith can be found in the book of Hebrews. Hebrews 11:1 states, "Now faith is confidence in what we hope for and assurance about what we do not see." It is a belief in something greater than yourself, to carry you through life, through both the good times and the bad times, and when you cannot see the way in front of you.

An example of the importance of family can be seen in I Kings 5:13-14, which states in part, "King Solomon conscripted laborers from all Israel – thirty thousand men. He sent them off to Lebanon in shifts of ten thousand a month, so that they spent one month in Lebanon and two months at home." King Solomon, in building the temple, arranged the schedules of the workers so that the workers would not have to be away from their families for long periods of time because he saw the strength in family that was needed to complete the goal of building the temple.

(Now that you have read this far, you are probably wondering how I am going to tie football into all this.)

An example of a verse that can be applied to football is Ecclesiastes 9:11, which states, "I have seen something else under the sun: The race is not to the swift or the battle to the strong, nor does food come to the wise or wealth to the brilliant or favor to the learned; but time and chance happen to them all." There are many intangibles that happen in the game of football that are out of the coaches' and players' control, such as the weather, the referees, injuries, etc. In our lives, we also deal with intangibles that happen over which we have no control. It is during those times, especially, that we feel our faith being tested. However, it is also during those times that we can draw strength and courage from our family and friends, and grow in our faith.

From the contest of football, we learn to never give up and to keep trying regardless of the score. In the same respect, in the game of life, we need to learn to work through our problems through the faith that we have and the strength that we draw from our family and friends. It is my hope for each and every one of us that we keep learning and growing together.

Blessings to all,
Chaplain Krupnik

My Musings

Light-

_____

_____

_____

_____

_____

_____

Life-

_____

_____

_____

_____

_____

_____

Lead-

_____

_____

_____

_____

_____

_____

_____

Taking Shortcuts

The other day, as I was returning from the Ontario airport, there was a traffic backup where I-215 and I-15 meet. I'm sure all of you are familiar with that location. I decided that I did not want to wait in the traffic, and exited off of the freeway, looking for a shortcut. The shortcut would have worked if it had not been for the two extremely long trains that crossed my path. I would have been better off staying with the traffic and waiting patiently.

There are times in our own lives when we feel that we are in a traffic jam waiting for God to answer our prayers. While we are waiting, we become impatient, and want to take a shortcut on our own. A classic example in the Old Testament is Abraham, who got impatient waiting for God to give him his promised son, and took things into his own hands by having a son with Sarah's maidservant, Hagar. Abraham's actions created more problems for him that he could have prevented if he had waited patiently for God.

When we take action into our own hands and follow our own will instead of God's will, we often create a mess. God tells us to wait on Him and not take things into our own hands. Psalm 37:7 states, "Be still before the Lord and wait patiently for him; do not fret when men succeed in their ways, when they carry out their wicked schemes." Let us remember when we get impatient waiting on God to be careful of the shortcuts that we might want to take, and instead, wait patiently on Him, because He is faithful.

Blessings to all,
Chaplain Krupnik

My Musings

Light-
_____

_____

_____

_____

_____

_____

Life-
_____

_____

_____

_____

_____

_____

Lead-
_____

_____

_____

_____

_____

_____

_____

Judging Others

During this past week, there have been headlines regarding the misconduct of leaders in our nation. People have asked me what is my opinion regarding these headlines. I would not give an opinion, because I do not know all of the facts. The Bible tells us to be careful about judging others.

Matthew 7:1-2 states, "Judge not that ye be not judged; for with what judgment ye judge, ye shall be judged: and with what measure ye mete, it shall be measured to you again." Christ is telling us to be careful in our judgment of others, because, in the same way that we judge others, we will be judged. "Judge not" is a prohibition against rash and hasty spiritual judgment. The prohibition is not against forming tentative opinions and evaluating facts. John 7:24 states, "Judge not according to the appearance, but judge righteous judgment." We are prohibited from making hasty and rash judgment that is not based on all of the facts. Proverbs 18:13 states, "He that answereth a matter before he heareth it, it is folly and shame unto him." Human judgment is partial and tentative. Final judgment belongs to God, and God alone. We are not to usurp God's judgment by our own.

By our own repentance, faith, confession, and obedience, we have enough struggles as individuals to worry about. Our energy would be better focused on our individual relationship with God rather than the judgment of others. Let us strive to focus on removing the "beam" in our own eye before we focus on the "splinter" in the eye of our brother or sister, because our final accounting is to God.

Blessings to all,
Chaplain Krupnik

My Musings

Light-
_____
_____
_____
_____
_____
_____

Life-
_____
_____
_____
_____
_____
_____

Lead-
_____
_____
_____
_____
_____
_____
_____

A Tribute

This week my daughter celebrated her eighteenth birthday. (Yahoo!) For myself and my wife, it was a time of celebration and reflection. For us, it is an end of responsibility. For her, it is just the beginning. As with all parents, we hope that we have done our best. I know that my wife and I have tried to do the best that we could have, and we will continue to help her along the way.

Turning eighteen is a time of transition for my daughter, as she looks forward to the future. As she is developing into a young woman, what kind of woman do we hope that she will be? Proverbs 31 gives many characteristics of a virtuous woman. Those characteristics include being trustworthy (vs. 11), benevolent (vs. 12), industrious (vs. 13-16), compassionate (vs. 17-19), having a good self-image (vs. 17-19), and having a constructive use of her speech (vs. 26). These traits, along with love as described in I Corinthians 13, are traits that we hope she will continue to develop throughout her life. I know that her mother and I both would like to echo the words of Proverbs 31:29 to her: "Many daughters have done virtuously, but thou excellest them all."

Blessings to all,
Chaplain Krupnik

My Musings

Light-

_____

_____

_____

_____

_____

Life-

_____

_____

_____

_____

_____

Lead-

_____

_____

_____

_____

_____

_____

Faith and Fog

The other day I was taking my wife to the Ontario airport, and we had to travel through the Cajon pass. At the time that we went through the pass, there was very thick fog. Because of the fog, visibility was down to the distance of a few car lengths.

In our own lives, situations occur like fog, unexpectedly and without warning. Because of those situations, our visibility becomes obscured as to how we see God. At times the fog can make us feel out of control, because we cannot see what lies ahead. God tells us, in Hebrews 13:5, "Never will I leave you; never will I forsake you." I knew, as I drove through the fog, that I had to slow down. I could not go as fast as I wanted to. Sometimes God puts fog in our lives to get us to slow down and to get our attention.

While traveling through the fog, a car passed us whose license plate said, "UCFAITH". Faith is what is necessary to guide us through the fog. The fog causes us to look to God in faith to help us through rather than relying on our own strength. Hebrews 11:1 states, "Now faith is being sure of what we hope for and certain of what we do not see." It is our faith that God has given us that will help us make it through the fog as we travel through the mountain passes of life. Let us remember to look to Him to guide us through the fog. Also, let us remember to look to Him when there is no fog so that He does not have to create fog to get our attention.

Blessings to all,
Chaplain Krupnik

My Musings

Light-
_____
_____
_____
_____
_____
_____

Life-
_____
_____
_____
_____
_____
_____

Lead-
_____
_____
_____
_____
_____
_____
_____

The Ghost of Past Sins

As we begin this year, it is a time to reflect on the past and to look forward to the future. I want to remind each of us, as we reflect, to remember God's grace that has been provided to us. I Peter 4:10 tells us, "As every man hath received the gift, even so minister the same one to another, as good stewards of the manifold grace of God." For that gift to be effective, we need to internalize it. We need to apply God's grace to ourselves to help us with our self-image (how we see ourselves).

When we commit an act of sin, we feel guilty. We go to God and ask for forgiveness. Because of His grace, God forgives. However, we often have a difficult time forgiving ourselves. God's grace is also available to help us deal with the remnants of guilt and the residue of shame. For me, shame is the ghost of past sins that have been forgiven, but yet seem to continue to haunt us. That is where God's grace comes into play. It is God's grace, through His Spirit, that deals with the ghosts of past sins that are forgiven. It is God's spirit of love and mercy that should give us that peace. However, we need to internalize that grace to deal with the ghosts of shame. God's forgiveness is not made complete in our lives until we are able to do that. Let us help each other to accomplish this in our lives by reminding each other as we think of the ghosts of shame that God has already taken that burden from us through His forgiveness and grace.

Blessings to all,
Chaplain Krupnik

My Musings

Light-

_____

_____

_____

_____

_____

_____

Life-

_____

_____

_____

_____

_____

_____

Lead-

_____

_____

_____

_____

_____

_____

_____

Images of a Call

I was driving on I-40 westbound from Needles last week during the rain showers. My son was looking at the cloud formations and told me that one of the formations of clouds looked like the clouds from the movie, "The Agony and the Ecstasy." In the movie, the images in the clouds looked like God and Adam reaching out to each other, and inspired Michaelangelo for the painting of the ceiling in the Sistine Chapel.

God reaches out to us in so many ways, calling us through His Spirit to have fellowship. What is our response to God when He calls us? We make a choice whether or not to respond. In Isaiah 6:8, Isaiah states, "Also I heard the voice of the Lord, saying, Whom shall I send, and who will go for us?" Regardless of the size of the crowd in which we find ourselves, when God speaks, it is on an individual basis. Isaiah realized that he was an audience of one. God is asking, who will yield to His call. God was asking Isaiah to be a part of the working of an invisible kingdom. God also asks us to be a part of that same work.

Isaiah's response to God was, "Here am I, send me." How do we respond today? When God is reaching out to us in the clouds, are we reaching out to Him, or turning the other way? Let us keep in mind His image and His call for our lives this day and every day.

Blessing to all,
Chaplain Krupnik

My Musings

Light-
_____

_____

_____

_____

_____

_____

Life-
_____

_____

_____

_____

_____

_____

Lead-
_____

_____

_____

_____

_____

_____

_____

Whaz u---------p?

No doubt a majority of you watched the football championship game, at least for a while. Some were watching it for the game; others were watching it for the commercials. I must admit that there was quite a variety of commercials. One of the most intriguing commercials was exploring the different ways that a person can say, "Whaz u---------p?"

God uses many different ways to ask us, "Whaz u--------p?" He uses his Spirit, his Word, our conscience, and other people. Matthew 6:8 states that your Father knows what you need before you ask him. Despite the knowledge that He has, God still wants us to come to Him in prayer about every aspect of our lives. God is concerned with what's up in our lives, and He wants to have fellowship with us. He is concerned about us in a very personal way. From now on, every time you see those commercials, remember that God is also asking you the same question.

Blessings to all,
Chaplain Krupnik

My Musings

Light-

_____

_____

_____

_____

_____

_____

Life-

_____

_____

_____

_____

_____

_____

Lead-

_____

_____

_____

_____

_____

_____

Our Walk with God

At the R.V. parking area located at the Marine Corps Logistics Base, many of the visitors have a ritual of walking in the morning and walking in the evening. They do it for a variety of reasons, including exercise, relaxation, and socializing for their pets.

From a spiritual perspective, God wants us to walk with him daily. We have some requirements for walking with God. We need to be reconciled to God. We need to be completely yielded to God. We need to love God supremely. We need to have unbroken fellowship with God.

Enoch walked with God. Genesis 5:24. Being reconciled to God implies trust, friendship, fellowship, companionship, and unity of thought. To be yielded to God requires us to give our mind and will over to God. God's thoughts become our thoughts. His teachings become our teachings. When we love God supremely, it keeps us focused on the correct purpose for our lives and restrains us from the popular sins of our day.

For us to have unbroken fellowship with God provides direction and comfort in our times of sorrow. Walking with God should be a daily ritual in our lives with practical application.

Blessings to all,
Chaplain Krupnik

My Musings

Light-
_____
_____
_____
_____
_____
_____

Life-
_____
_____
_____
_____
_____
_____

Lead-
_____
_____
_____
_____
_____
_____
_____

The Agony of Defeat

Most of you remember the phrase made famous by a major news network in the coverage of sports, "The thrill of victory and the agony of defeat." We experienced the agony of defeat this past weekend, as my daughter's basketball team lost in the state playoffs by one point in double overtime to the team that will probably win the state championship for their level.

As we journey through this life, we encounter victories and defeats, physically and spiritually. Handling victory does not seem to be as difficult as handling defeat. I believe that in part defeat is difficult because any time we compete in anything, we take a risk. In any challenge, we risk being defeated. However, for anything to improve in our lives, we need to take some sort of risk no matter how small.

The Bible tells us to put our faith and trust in God and to go forward in our lives, even if it involves taking a risk. Philippians 3:13-14 states, "Brothers, I do not consider myself yet to have taken hold of it. But one thing I do: Forgetting what is behind and straining toward what is ahead, I press on toward the goal to win the prize for which God has called me heavenward in Christ Jesus." Whether you have had many victories or many defeats in your past, this verse applies to all. Forget those things which are behind and press forward with God.

Blessings to all,
Chaplain Krupnik

My Musings

Light-

_____

_____

_____

_____

_____

_____

Life-

_____

_____

_____

_____

_____

_____

Lead-

_____

_____

_____

_____

_____

_____

_____

Celebrate Life

This past week I took my two youngest sons to the pizza place with the giant mouse. My two youngest children are a teenager and a preteen. They still enjoy going there. I observed that all of the people that were there came to have fun, to celebrate living, and to celebrate relationships of friends and family. It was a reminder to me that we need to take the time to celebrate the relationships that we have been given by God and have fun and enjoy the life that we have together.

Philippians 2:2 states, "Fulfill ye my joy, that ye be likeminded, having the same love, being of one accord, of one mind." For us to enjoy the relationship fully, we have to be likeminded. What peace, joy, and fulfillment we can have when we are of one love, one accord, and one mind in our relationships. We need to take and make the time to develop the relationships in our lives.

Blessings to all,
Chaplain Krupnik

My Musings

Light- _____

_____

_____

_____

_____

_____

Life- _____

_____

_____

_____

_____

_____

Lead- _____

_____

_____

_____

_____

_____

_____

Patterns of Behavior

I was sitting in my car waiting for a store to open when another car pulled up next to me and parked in the handicapped parking space. The person driving (the only person in the vehicle) reached down and pulled out the handicapped parking permit and hung it on the mirror. When the store opened, the person got out of the vehicle to go into the store. No physical impairment was visible. In fact, the person was walking better than I do. I thought to myself how selfish this person's actions were.

What makes a person act in such a manner? Is there a pattern of behavior that develops? Granted, I do not have all of the facts, but it appears that this person was doing something selfish and illegal. Proverbs tells us as a dog returns to its vomit, so a fool does to his folly.

In our own lives, we develop patterns of behavior that we have justified to be okay when in reality the behavior is not okay or appropriate. If such behavior is left unchecked in our lives, we will probably develop patterns of behavior that are worse for our lives and the lives of those around us. It is my hope that if we love someone, we will take the steps necessary to get rid of those patterns of behavior. We need to make ourselves accountable to someone else to help us get rid of those little behavior patterns that we need to correct so that they do not turn into a big problem.

We should all take the time to evaluate our actions and patterns of behavior to determine if we might be doing something wrong that could be hurtful to others.

Blessings to all,
Chaplain Krupnik

My Musings

Light- _____
_____
_____
_____
_____
_____
_____

Life- _____
_____
_____
_____
_____
_____

Lead- _____
_____
_____
_____
_____
_____
_____
_____

Warning, No Lines Painted

As I was driving home to Phoenix this past weekend late at night, a flashing road sign alerted me that road construction was ahead and that no lines were painted on the road. The yellow and white lines on the road are important because they tell us the lanes that we are in on the highway, set the boundaries, and tell us when we can pass. It was interesting and at times scary to be traveling down a highway late at night with no boundaries and no guidance. It made me realize how important those lines and boundaries are for protection and for safety for myself and others. I had taken those lines for granted.

I thought about the lines and boundaries (laws, regulations, orders, ethics) that are the boundaries, the painted lines that govern our lives. The purpose of those lines is to protect me and to protect others. Without those lines in my life, my life would be without order; rather, it would be chaos. Proverbs 2:6-8 states, "For the Lord gives wisdom and from his mouth come knowledge and understanding. He holds victory in store for the upright, he is a shield to those whose walk is blameless, for he guards the course of the just and protects the way of his faithful ones." We need to ensure that our lines are based on God's wisdom, because that will create balance in our lives and guide us in the direction that God wants us to go. Without that guidance and balance, we will get off of the road that we should be on and lose our way. Let us remember to look to the true source of guidance to make sure that we are walking within the right lines.

Blessings to all,
Chaplain Krupnik

My Musings

Light- _____

_____

_____

_____

_____

_____

Life- _____

_____

_____

_____

_____

_____

_____

Lead- _____

_____

_____

_____

_____

_____

_____

_____

Dead Plants, New Roots

My wife called me the other day to tell me that some flowers that she had planted several years ago (which had died) had bloomed again after the recent rains. Those flowers made me think of our spiritual lives. At times, it feels like our spiritual lives have become dead. I do not believe that our spiritual lives become dead, but they may become dormant. We need to look for rain for our spiritual lives to bloom again. The rain of forgiveness, grace, understanding, compassion, acceptance, etc., are all things that we need to experience to grow spiritually. God promises us forgiveness if we come to Him. Psalm 130:3-4 states, "If you, O Lord, kept a record of our sins, O Lord, who could stand? But with you there is forgiveness; therefore you are feared." It is never too late to bloom again, but we need to go where the rain is for us to grow. It is my hope and prayer that we will all seek the rain to grow.

Blessings to all,
Chaplain Krupnik

My Musings

Light- _____

_____

_____

_____

_____

_____

Life- _____

_____

_____

_____

_____

_____

Lead- _____

_____

_____

_____

_____

_____

_____

The Exercise of Grace

I was coming back to the base from Ft. Irwin one evening last week. It had been a long day and I was tired, listening to the radio and not paying attention to my speed (it was not excessive but it was over the limit), when all of a sudden, a red spotlight from out of the darkness caught my sight. It was a peace officer giving me a warning to slowdown. The officer used discretion in the situation to alert me to my speeding. I am thankful that the officer exercised discretion. That discretion can also be called grace.

The Bible talks about grace as an undeserved favor or gift from God. Romans 3:2324 states, "For all have sinned and fall short of the glory of GOD, and are justified freely by his grace through the redemption that came by Christ Jesus." As God applied His grace to us, we can apply that grace to others. Practice a little grace with one another this week.

Blessings to all,
Chaplain Krupnik

My Musings

Light-

_____

_____

_____

_____

_____

Life-

_____

_____

_____

_____

_____

Lead-

_____

_____

_____

_____

_____

_____

Sharing the Load

I have been watching a show on television over the last few months on a regular basis. The show involves two teams that compete with each other over building a certain item out of materials in a junkyard; I'm sure you know the name of the show. When I was first asked to watch the show, I had my reservations. However, I got hooked and now I look forward to watching the show. I think it is because deep down inside, it appeals to the tinkerer, the mechanic, the builder of Lincoln logs, Legos, shop class, etc. I also think we identify with the individuals working together as a team, putting their ideas together, to create the final product.

When we work together for a common goal and purpose, we share each other's burdens. Galatians 6:2 tells us to "carry each other's burdens, and in this way you will fulfill the law of Christ." Each day we are given a task: to live our lives to the fullest for God. Many times that day can be heavy with burdens. Let us share the load with each other and make the burden lighter.

Blessings to all,
Chaplain Krupnik

My Musings

Light-

_____

_____

_____

_____

_____

_____

Life-

_____

_____

_____

_____

_____

_____

Lead-

_____

_____

_____

_____

_____

_____

_____

After the Seed is Planted

One can tell that it is Spring, even in the desert, by the new plant life all around. The area around our chapel is full of beautiful flowers, thanks to the constant devotion of one of our parishioners. She is constantly feeding, watering, and weeding those flowers. Her hard work is paying off, as those flowers have taken root and now are in full bloom.

Our spiritual lives are like those flowers. For us to grow and bloom spiritually, we must be fed and watered. How can we be fed? By spending time in God's Word, in prayer, and with God's people. Psalm 34:8 states, 'Taste and see that the Lord is good." To do that, we need to spend time with Him.

Our spiritual lives also need to be weeded. God often refers to sin in our lives as weeds that come up and try to choke out the good. We need to be open to God so that we can see the weeds in our lives and allow God to pull them so we can grow.

I hope that each of us will allow God to feed us and pull the weeds in our lives today so that we can grow in Him.

Blessings to all,
Chaplain Krupnik

My Musings

Light-

_____

_____

_____

_____

_____

_____

Life-

_____

_____

_____

_____

_____

_____

_____

Lead-

_____

_____

_____

_____

_____

_____

_____

Open to Ownership

I'm sure that many of you have a favorite pet or pets. Our pet is a miniature schnauzer, by the name of Panzer. Panzer is always there to meet each one of us when we come home, and he is just as happy to see us if we have been gone five minutes as if we have been gone for five days. He loves to give out affection and seems to know when a person is feeling down. He loves to serve his owner.

Panzer's faithfulness, love, devotion and affection towards his owner makes me think about the unconditional love relationship that I have with my God. Spiritually, God is the owner of our spirit, and it is through that relationship of the spirit that God wants us to always try to be joyful and happy in that relationship regardless of the circumstances. It makes me think about in everything that I do, and in all of the circumstances that I am involved in, am I glad to have God in that relationship? Philippians 4:4 states, "Rejoice in the Lord always. I will say it again: Rejoice!" Are we always welcoming God's presence in our lives?

God tells us that He will never leave us or forsake us. There have been times in my life when I was searching for and doubting the presence and existence of God in my life. In reality, what I was doing was not being open to His presence, open to His ownership of my spirit, open to the ownership that God has of my life. This does not mean that the relationship that we have with God comes easy for us. Many times it comes with difficulty. However, as we mature in our lives, we begin to understand that the relationship that we have with God in our lives grows in value as God works with us through those difficulties.

As we go through life, let us remember to be open to and rejoice in the relationship that we have with God.

Blessings to all,
Chaplain Krupnik

My Musings

Light-
_____
_____
_____
_____
_____
_____

Life-
_____
_____
_____
_____
_____
_____

Lead-
_____
_____
_____
_____
_____
_____
_____

Handling Anger

I was driving back the other day from Phoenix on a hot day and it was uncomfortable. I realized after a few hours of driving how irritated I had become over little things, like traffic, people, etc. The temperature increase had influenced my emotions in a negative way. I am sure a biological reason exists and keeping cool physically is one way to handle it. But sometimes we cannot be in a cool place at work, home, or when we are traveling. When we are in those circumstances, we need to address those feelings and speak honestly to God about them. If we express our feelings to God, we can deal with those feelings without exploding in harsh words and actions, possibly hurting ourselves and others. We read in Job 7:11, "Therefore I will not keep silent; I will speak out in the anguish of my spirit, I will complain in the bitterness of my soul." Job spoke openly about his emotions regarding the circumstances he was facing. As Job knew, God can handle our anger.

The next time strong emotions threaten to overwhelm you, express them openly to God in prayer. This will help you gain a perspective on the situation and give you greater ability to deal with it constructively.

Blessings to all,
Chaplain Krupnik

My Musings

Light- _____

_____

_____

_____

_____

_____

_____

Life- _____

_____

_____

_____

_____

_____

_____

Lead- _____

_____

_____

_____

_____

_____

_____

_____

Backward and Forward

I was home a week ago to attend my daughter's high school graduation. It was a joyous day and a sad day. I was so glad to see her graduate. She walked with confidence and freedom across the stage to receive her diploma.

During these times one looks backward and forward about a life with someone and what that person means to you. Of course, reality comes back very quickly. However, during that time of reflection I remembered certain events of my daughter growing up and becoming a young lady. All of the effort, concern, and worry was worth it. The reflection was not idealistic but I realized the value of the relationship that I have with my daughter and I hope that she values the relationship with her dad.

Each and every one of us has value with God the Father. At this point we have not graduated. We are still in school, learning as we go, until one day we graduate to eternal life. The journey through the school of life at times seems like a never ending process .We ask at times, "Are we there yet?" The answer, of course, is "No, not yet."

The life we live at times seems to be a mystery. How I made it through 18 years with my daughter is a mystery. Time goes by so fast when you look back on it. In the same way, the relationship that we have with God is a mystery at times. In Ephesians 3, Paul talks about the mystery of the Gospel and how the purpose for all is to be able to approach God with freedom and confidence. That freedom and confidence comes from believing and having faith in God.

Let us live our lives with that freedom and confidence in the Gospel, and keep striving in our faith until graduation day.

Blessings to all,
Chaplain Krupnik

My Musings

Light- _____

_____

_____

_____

_____

_____

Life- _____

_____

_____

_____

_____

_____

Lead- _____

_____

_____

_____

_____

_____

_____

Our Identity

I attended a luncheon some time ago in our community. One of the items of informal discussion at the luncheon related to with having identity in our community. Someone remarked that he liked the community because people know who he was; he was not just one of many. It was a reminder that we all want identity. We all want to be someone that is accepted and welcomed in the community no matter where it is, whether at home, work, school, or church.

Spiritually we have an identity in our faith. But what do we do with that identity in our faith? Do we allow that identity in our faith through the Spirit of God to be a part of who we are? Is that identity only when we worship, or do we carry it with us all the time joyfully, or is it at times a struggle? It is a struggle between our old nature and new nature, a struggle between actions of righteousness and unrighteousness. If we truly identify with our faith, then we should be identifying with righteousness. Our actions should reflect what we believe in. It is a challenge. The challenge is made easier when we recommit ourselves to the identity of our faith and ask God to help us live that identity of righteousness. Romans 8:26-27 states, "In the same way, the Spirit helps us in weakness. We do not know what we ought to pray for, but the Spirit himself intercedes for us with groans that words cannot express and he who searches our hearts knows the mind of the Spirit, because the Spirit intercedes for the saints in accordance with God's will." Help is present for each and every one of us in the spiritual identity we have in our faith. We have to want that help and seek it for it to be a part of who we are and what we want to become.

Blessings to all,
Chaplain Krupnik

My Musings

Light-
_____
_____
_____
_____
_____
_____
_____

Life-
_____
_____
_____
_____
_____
_____
_____

Lead-
_____
_____
_____
_____
_____
_____
_____

The Core of Independence

The celebration of July 4th historically is the acceptance by the Continental Congress of the Proclamation, The Declaration of Independence, on July 4, 1776. The Declaration of Independence stated the reasons for independence from Great Britain.

The memories of the 4th of July are time spent in relationships with family and friends, celebrating with events such as fireworks (legal ones, of course), picnics, parades, concerts, and time with family and friends. The core of those relationships is spending leisure time being oneself and accepting others for themselves.

Although independence is a wonderful thing, within families there should also be interdependence. We should build each other up within our families, and be able to share both our burdens and our joys. Otherwise, we feel alone and lost, like a sheep without a shepherd.

In the same respect, our relationship with God and the church should be a relationship of interdependence, rather than independence. John 10:14 states, "I am the Good Shepherd; I know my sheep and my sheep know me." We know each other within our flock because of the time we spend together. We have to spend time with God or else our independent ways will seek relationships that will make us stray away from God, and we will become lost and confused. Spend time with God and be founded in that relationship. As we spend time with God, and follow His will, we will know that we belong to Him, and will see His way for our lives.

Blessings to all,
Chaplain Krupnik

My Musings

Light-

_____

_____

_____

_____

_____

_____

Life-

_____

_____

_____

_____

_____

_____

Lead-

_____

_____

_____

_____

_____

_____

_____

The Value of our Loyalty

I went shopping the other day in one of the local stores. Most items listed had two prices: one price was the regular price and the other price was the valued customer price. To receive the valued customer price, a person was required to sign up for the valued customer card. Many stores have similar programs to compete for the customer. The purpose of such programs is to develop customer loyalty and return business.

Our loyalty is sought after in all relationships of our lives. All relationships require us to be loyal, and we require loyalty in return. Loyalty means commitment, focus, respect, affection, adoration, selflessness, etc.

Sometimes our loyalty is not repaid to us in the way that we want it to be. We feel as though others are taking advantage of us. What is our responsibility in that situation? We are still to be loyal. Why are we still to be loyal, you may ask. For the long haul in this experience of life that we have been given, we will be better off as individuals if we fulfill our commitment of loyalty. By staying loyal to our commitment, we are in control of the situation instead of the situation controlling us. Romans 8:28 tells us, "And we know that in all things God works for the good of those who love him who have been called according to his purpose." This verse is not a copout, but a practical response of the loyalty that we are to have to God. It is in that relationship with God that we truly find what is primary in our loyalty. When we understand that, other events in our lives are secondary, because we realize that our primary responsibility is our loyalty to God (because of His loyalty to us). This loyalty gives us the strength spirituality to deal with the unexpected difficulties that we have in life. Each day we face with confidence and hope not fear because of the value of the spiritual we have between ourselves and God.

Blessings to all,
Chaplain Krupnik

My Musings

Light-

_____

_____

_____

_____

_____

Life-

_____

_____

_____

_____

_____

Lead-

_____

_____

_____

_____

_____

A Vow of Trust

The other day I went with my son to see the movie, "Planet of the Apes." One of the main plots in the movie was trust. That trust was portrayed in different ways. One of the obvious ways that it was portrayed was when one of the apes had to go across water. (As portrayed in the movie, apes are afraid of water – they don't know how to swim). One of the human characters reassured the ape with a vow of trust that he would not let her drown.

In our own lives, many times we look for reassurance and trust from God because of our fears. It is our spiritual relationship with God that can provide for us the strength we need to give us spiritual confidence and overcome our fears. God has vowed to us that if we put our trust in Him, He will be trustworthy to us for everything in our lives. How do we respond to that trust? Do we go forward in our lives because of that trust or do we choose to remain stagnant and even, sometimes, go backwards in our lives because of our fears.

God tell us that He does not give us a life of fear, but of power, and of love, and a sound mind. II Timothy 1:7. For our trust in God to be made complete, God gives us a free will to choose whether or not to trust Him. When we choose to trust God in everything, we demonstrate our faith in Him. Many of the fears that we struggle with in our lives are because we have chosen not to trust God. When we choose to not trust God with the circumstances in our lives, we drown in our own fears spiritually and emotionally. God is reaching out to us right now, asking us to trust in Him. It is my hope that each and every one of us will put our trust and confidence in this life and in the life yet to come in God.

Blessings to all,
Chaplain Krupnik

My Musings

Light-

_____

_____

_____

_____

_____

_____

Life-

_____

_____

_____

_____

_____

_____

Lead-

_____

_____

_____

_____

_____

_____

_____

Going the Distance

I was in San Diego last weekend and saw a marathon race taking place in the downtown area. The runners varied in terms of ability, but all had a goal to start the race and to finish it. I am sure that many of the runners were feeling personal pain from the grueling nature of the race. However, the runners persevered despite the pain. How the runners finished was based on their individual abilities and amount of training in preparation for the race. All had a goal and some sort of motivation for participation in the race.

Spiritually, our race with God is a marathon. It is a relationship race for the long term. Do we want to participate in the race? What is our motivation? What effort do we make in preparation? What is our goal in our relationship with God? How we see ourselves spiritually determines those answers. Are we committed to the spiritual race with God?

Hebrews 12:1-2 states, "Therefore, since we are surrounded by such a great cloud of witnesses, let us throw off everything that hinders and the sin that so easily entangles, and let us run with perseverance the race marked out for us. Let us fix our eyes on Jesus, the author and perfecter of our faith, who for the joy set before him endured the cross, scorning its shame, and sat down at the right hand of the throne of God." Like the marathon runner, our relationship with God should be for the long term. That long term goal requires us to be committed in the relationship. Sometimes we fail to see that God is with us on the long race because we focus so much on the personal pain of each step versus our commitment to God in completing the race. During the good times and bad times, we need to remember that God is always there with us in the race, and will help us to accomplish the long term goal.

Blessings to all,
Chaplain Krupnik

My Musings

Light- _____

_____

_____

_____

_____

_____

Life- _____

_____

_____

_____

_____

_____

Lead- _____

_____

_____

_____

_____

_____

_____

Sacrifices

I attended a meeting last week in San Diego where the guest speaker was John Finn, the most senior living medal of honor recipient by date of action, December 7, 1941. Mr. Finn stated that he was just doing his job on that day. His actions, of course, were much more than just doing his job. What impressed me about him was his remembrance by name of his fellow shipmates who made the ultimate sacrifice on that day. Because of those sacrifices, and the sacrifices of others, we enjoy our salvation of freedom.

Do we remember the sacrifices that have made our spiritual salvation possible? Do we value the salvation that we have obtained? For us to appreciate the value of our salvation, we need to share it with others. It is shared in our attitudes and actions. The value of our salvation is shared by how we live our lives. We honor the sacrifice of salvation by sharing it, by living it. If we do not share it and live it, it really has no value to us.

We have God's protection with us in our spiritual battles when we are just doing our jobs as followers of Him. Ephesians 6:13 states, "Therefore put on the full armor of God, so that when the day of evil comes, you may be able to stand your ground, and after you have done everything, to stand." God's armor includes the belt of truth, the breastplate of righteousness, feet fitted with the gospel of peace, the shield of faith, the helmet of salvation, and the sword of the Spirit. Let's use these tools to live the salvation that God has given to us.

Blessings to all,
Chaplain Krupnik

My Musings

Light-

_____

_____

_____

_____

_____

_____

Life-

_____

_____

_____

_____

_____

_____

Lead-

_____

_____

_____

_____

_____

_____

_____

Every Life Has a Story

I was watching television this week when a commercial came on about a publication that tells true stories about famous people. The commercial had a subtitle that said, "Every life has a story." Each and every one of us has a story about our own life. My story or your story may not be a famous one, but it has value in the eyes of God. The story of our life should include a relationship with God. A relationship with God that reveals in us how precious God is in our life. We demonstrate the story of that relationship in all that we do.

What does my story say about that relationship? It tells that I have made mistakes in that relationship, that more times than not I want my own way. The story also reveals how time and time again I realize how important my relationship is with God and I keep returning. God keeps taking me back because my story, just like your story, is so important to Him. Hebrews 12:14 tells us, "Make every effort to live in peace with all men and to be holy; without holiness no one will see the Lord." Our story with God needs to include the effort to live in peace and holiness so that others may see the Lord. In spite of ourselves, let us make every effort to include God in the story of our lives. One day when our stories are revealed, it can be said, "Well done, thou good and faithful servant."

Blessings to all,
Chaplain Krupnik

My Musings

Light-

_____

_____

_____

_____

_____

_____

Life-

_____

_____

_____

_____

_____

_____

Lead-

_____

_____

_____

_____

_____

_____

_____

Our Purpose in Living

I attended a memorial service this week. One part of the service was the eulogy. The eulogy was given by the son. The son paid tribute to his father and the relationship they had together. The son focused his tribute on the value of his father's service to his family, nation, community and church.

The focus of his fathers' life was that of service for others. What greater purpose is there in our lives than service?

In the gospel of Matthew, chapter 16, verse 25, we read, "For whoever wants to save his life will lose it, but whoever loses his life for me will find it." Our spiritual discipleship requires us to make a real commitment of service. That commitment of service gives a purpose in our lives in all that we do. I believe we can lose our intended purpose when we do not have a commitment to service in our lives. Without that purpose of service, we become selfish, territorial, negative etc.. When we have that commitment to service, our purpose becomes just the opposite. We want what benefits others. We see a greater good other than ourselves. Our witness of discipleship is seen and draws others to have that same relationship with God. What we will discover in our service is our real purpose in living, which is our service to each other.

Blessings to all,
Chaplain Krupnik

My Musings

Light-
_____
_____
_____
_____
_____
_____

Life-
_____
_____
_____
_____
_____
_____

Lead-
_____
_____
_____
_____
_____
_____
_____

Justice in God's Time

I was watching the movie, "Moby Dick," this week. The story of "Moby Dick" is basically the consuming nature of revenge. Revenge in the story clouded the judgment of one individual. Because of that clouded judgment, innocent lives were lost and the main purpose of the individual failed.

The events of these past two weeks have caused a variety of emotions in all of us. I believe that all of us are looking for justice. The justice we are seeking needs to include a spiritual reflection from God – God's justice. In Isaiah 61:8, God says, "For I the Lord love justice. I hate robbery and iniquity." Justice is rendering to everyone that which is his due.

Isaiah 28:17 states, "I shall use justice as a plumb-line and righteousness as a plummet." I believe that our focus should be to do all possible to bring about justice and not revenge. If we seek revenge, it will cloud our judgment and our ability to distinguish right from wrong, just like in Moby Dick, where innocent lives were lost and the main purpose for the voyage failed when revenge consumed Captain Ahab. In the heart-felt emotions that we have about the events in the last two weeks, we need to include justice and not revenge to balance those emotions. After we have done all that is possible, the situation needs to be placed in God's hands and the outcome left with him.

Blessings to all,
Chaplain Krupnik

My Musings

Light-

_____

_____

_____

_____

_____

_____

Life-

_____

_____

_____

_____

_____

_____

Lead-

_____

_____

_____

_____

_____

_____

_____

The Golden Rule

I was recently asked to give the opening prayer at the Kiwanis Club of Barstow's annual Installation of Officers and Board. This was my first exposure to the Kiwanis Club organization. I was very impressed with the organization's dedication to service in the community.

One of the "Objects of Kiwanis" is "To encourage the daily living of the Golden Rule in all human relationships." The Golden Rule is the name usually given to the command of Jesus recorded in Matthew 7:12 and Luke 6:31: "Do to others as you would like them to do to you." (This is not to be confused with the worldly version: Do unto others, then split.)

The designation, "Golden Rule," does not appear in the Bible, and its origin in English is difficult to trace. The principle of the Golden Rule, however, can be found throughout history in other religions. It was a common teaching in the Jewish book of Tobit, in the teaching of the early Jewish teacher, Hillel, and in Greek sources as well. The Old Testament also has references to this principle. Leviticus 19:18 states, "Do not seek revenge or bear a grudge against one of your people, but love your neighbor as yourself. I am the Lord."

Although this saying appears elsewhere in history, Jesus adds a twist. In other religions, the principle is stated negatively. "Don't do to others what you don't want done to you." Jesus, however, changes the statement into a positive principle, which makes it much more significant. It is not very hard to refrain from harming others; it is much more difficult to take the initiative to do something good for someone else. The Golden Rule, as Jesus formulated it, is the foundation of active goodness and mercy – the kind of love God shows to us every day. The application of the Golden Rule cannot be applied with judgment as to whether it is deserved or not. It can only be done in an act of service that is given freely, without expectation of getting anything in return.

As you go throughout your day, think of how you can apply the Golden Rule to your life, and look at what good actions you can take to benefit others.

Blessings to all,
Chaplain Krupnik

My Musings

Light- _____

_____

_____

_____

_____

_____

_____

Life- _____

_____

_____

_____

_____

_____

_____

Lead- _____

_____

_____

_____

_____

_____

_____

_____

Making Choices

I have attended several ceremonies this month acknowledging promotions in rank, awards for achievement, and the receiving of diplomas for educational accomplishments. It benefits our community to have these ceremonies because they publicly acknowledge the successful completion of goals set by the individuals involved. Acknowledging this completion of goals improves our community by making others set goals for themselves.

Those rewarded made an active choice to accomplish a goal. All of us should have goals in our lives. What goal do we set for ourselves spiritually? How do we measure the success of that goal? We can and do acknowledge external accomplishments of our spiritual commitment, i.e. worship attendance, offerings, active participation with our faith group etc. But what about the internal? We make an active internal spiritual choice daily by our actions. The Bible in Joshua 24:15 says, "But if serving the Lord seems undesirable to you, then choose for yourselves this day whom you will serve, whether the gods your forefathers served beyond the River or the gods of the Amorites in whose land you are living. But as for me and my household we will serve the Lord." In our choices we are revealing the spiritual goal for that day by what we think, do and say.

How do we make the proper choice in serving God daily? We have to desire it. We have to want it. We have to be open to the leading of the Spirit of God in our lives, to the truths and teachings that God has given us through our faith. Through the combination of all these things and more, we can make the proper choice in whom we will serve. Let our goal be this day and every day to serve the Lord.

Blessings to all,
Chaplain Krupnik

My Musings

Light-

_____

_____

_____

_____

_____

Life-

_____

_____

_____

_____

_____

Lead-

_____

_____

_____

_____

_____

_____

Our Children, Our Heritage

I recently attended a luncheon for Hispanic Heritage Month. The theme of the luncheon was, "Children, Our Hope for the Future."

Along the walls of the room were pictures of the children and relatives of employees at the Marine Corps Logistics Base. Each picture was accompanied by a short biography of the person's successes. I thought, what a great way to celebrate one's heritage!

The Bible discusses our heritage. Psalm 127:3 states, "Children are a heritage from the Lord, children a reward from him. Like arrows in the hands of a warrior are children born in one's youth. Blessed is the man whose quiver is full of them."

Our children are our legacy. It is my hope as parents that we build on our heritage to work to give our children a better life than we have had just as previous generations have done for us. As we work, fight, and struggle for better opportunities for our children, our community as a whole improves.

In addition to providing our children with an earthly heritage, we need to provide them with a spiritual heritage. I Peter 2:5 states, "You also, like living stones, are being built into a spiritual house to be a holy priesthood offering spiritual sacrifices acceptable to God through Jesus Christ." We have a spiritual heritage of our faith in Good that needs to be passed on to our children. Our children will not be complete until they receive both our earthly heritage and our spiritual heritage. It is never too late to start a spiritual heritage, to develop a relationship with God to pass on to our children.

I hope that each of you develops a relationship with God to enable you to pass on both your earthly heritage and your spiritual heritage to your children. Both need to be passed on and strengthened in our children for our community to improve.

Blessings to all,
Chaplain Krupnik

My Musings

Light- _____

_____

_____

_____

_____

_____

Life- _____

_____

_____

_____

_____

_____

Lead- _____

_____

_____

_____

_____

_____

_____

A Righteous Tree

The base has been cutting down diseased and dying trees over the last several months. I was watching the process this weekend and was amazed at the time and hard work it takes to cut down a tree.

The Bible uses the tree to represent different aspects of our life spiritually. In the book of Proverbs, it is referred to four times as a "tree of life." Proverbs 11:30 states, "The fruit of righteous is a tree of life and he who wins souls is wise." Living in the High Desert, a tree is appreciated because of its shade that it offers and a symbol of life that it represents. When we practice righteousness in our everyday lives, it is appreciated by those around us and it offers a symbol of goodness and hope in a world that has at times gone bad. When we continue to practice being righteous, we grow spiritually and become stronger in our faith. Our roots are grounded in serving God and establishing a practice of worship and dedication. The living water that we receive in the spirit of God helps us to grow and become strong. As we grow in God, it takes a lot of hard work and time to cut us down.

Let all of us make it a practice to be righteous (doing what is good) for each other as we serve God together.

Blessings to all,
Chaplain Krupnik

My Musings

Light-

_____
_____
_____
_____
_____
_____

Life-

_____
_____
_____
_____
_____
_____

Lead-

_____
_____
_____
_____
_____
_____

The Spiritual Factor

This past week I attended two events that reminded me that throughout our lives we should help those around us that are in need. The Mojave Valley Volunteer Hospice sponsored one event, and the Disabled Employee Awareness Program at Marine Corps Logistics Base sponsored the second event. Both events dealt with awareness of a need: one with cancer and the second with disability. Each need required a human factor to help improve the quality of life of the individuals in the community.

What factors do we allow to influence us when it comes to helping others? Do we allow the spiritual factor, including the Greatest Commandment, to influence us? When asked, "Teacher, which is the greatest commandment in the Law," Jesus replied, "Love the Lord your God with all your heart and with all your soul and with all your mind. This is the first and greatest commanded. And the second is like it: Love your neighbor as yourself. All the Law and the prophets hang on these two commandments." Matthew 22:36-40

When we allow the spiritual factor in our life to be a part of us, a transformation process begins, and our God begins to mold us spiritually.

A liturgical poet from the 10th Century, expanding on Jeremiah's imagery of God being the potter, wrote these words:

As clay are we, as soft and yielding clay
That lies between the fingers of the potter.
At his will he moulds it thick or thin,
And forms its shape according to his fancy.
So are we in Thy hand, God of love;
Thy covenant recall and show Thy mercy.

As stone are we, inert, resistless stone
That lies within the fingers of the mason.
At his will he keeps it firm and whole,
Or at his will he keeps it firm and whole,
Or at his pleasure hews it into fragments.
So are we in Thy hand, God of life;
Thy covenant recall and show Thy mercy.

The benefit we receive from helping others is a peace, a contentment, a satisfaction that wealth or position cannot provide. Let us endeavor to put into practice in our lives the spiritual factor as God continues the process of molding us and making us according to His will.

Blessings to all,
Chaplain Krupnik

My Musings

Light-
_____
_____
_____
_____
_____
_____

Life-
_____
_____
_____
_____
_____
_____

Lead-
_____
_____
_____
_____
_____
_____
_____

The Joy of the Lord

This week I went to a movie that just came out about the power source of scaring little children. However, at the conclusion of the movie, it was realized that a greater power source came from the laughter of little children.

In our spiritual lives, we have a great power source of living joyfully in our relationship with God. In Psalm 4:6-8 we read, "Many are asking, 'Who can show us any good?' Let the light of your face shine upon us, O Lord. You have filled my heart with greater joy than when their grain and new wine abound. I will lie down and sleep in peace for you alone, O Lord make me dwell in safety." Two kinds of joy are contrasted here; inward joy that comes from knowing and trusting God, and happiness that comes as a result of pleasant circumstances. Inward joy defeats discouragement; happiness covers it up. Inward joy is lasting; happiness is temporary.

Joy is a common theme in Jesus's teachings. He wants us to be joyful. In John 15:10-11 we read, "If you obey my commands, you will remain in my love, just as I have obeyed my Father's commands and remain in his love. I have told you this so that my joy may be in you and that your joy may be complete." The key to immeasurable joy is living in a close relationship with God, the source of all joy . When we do, we will experience God's special care and protection and see the victory God brings even when defeat seems certain in our lives spiritually. Let us rejoice in the Lord always and live on the power source of that joy in knowing God.

Blessings to all,
Chaplain Krupnik

My Musings

Light- _____

_____

_____

_____

_____

_____

_____

Life- _____

_____

_____

_____

_____

_____

_____

Lead- _____

_____

_____

_____

_____

_____

_____

Celebrate Life Through God

The Marine Corps celebrated its 225th birthday on November 10. At the birthday ball I attended for Marine Corps Logistics Base, Col. Mark A. Costa, base commander, gave the opening remarks for the celebration. One of the remarks Col. Costa made was that celebrating an event such as the Marine Corps birthday gives it life.

Any time we celebrate or remember an event, we put life into it. The life we give through the celebration is a life that sustains the tradition, the heritage and the legacy of the past, present and future.

For our spiritual life to keep living and thriving, we need to celebrate as often as we can in an act of worship. Whether we worship in public or private, the key is we need to be involved in worship.

Psalm 95:1 states, "Come let us sing for joy to the Lord; let us shout aloud to the Rock of our salvation." Our spiritual life cannot go on living unless we take an active role in worship through our individual relationship with God. We must be willing to be personally involved in worship to allow God to reveal His truth to us, about both Himself and ourselves.

Psalm 96:1-3 states, "Sing to the Lord a new song; sing to the Lord all the earth. Sing to the Lord, praise His name; proclaim His salvation day after day. Declare His glory among the nations, declare His marvelous deeds among all people." Let us continue to celebrate life as it has been given to us as a gift. Let us also remember to celebrate the spiritual life God has given to us by worshiping the Creator of that life. When we celebrate our relationship with God and with each other, it is a reminder to us to not take life, or the many blessings that we have been given, for granted.

Blessings to all,
Chaplain Krupnik

My Musings

Light-

_____

_____

_____

_____

_____

Life-

_____

_____

_____

_____

_____

Lead-

_____

_____

_____

_____

_____

_____

_____

Be a Real Turkey

It is my prayer that all had a good Thanksgiving. I attended a large gathering of family and friends. All of us brought different items for the meal. One of the many items, of course, was turkey. There was a difference in the real turkey meat and an imitation version that was supposed to be turkey meat. It looked good in appearance, but once a person tasted it, that person realized that the meat was not real.

The lives that we live in our faith are to be real, not just an outward appearance. We become real in our spiritual lives by making God a part of our lives. Psalm 34:8 tells us, "O taste and see that the Lord is good! Happy is the man who takes refuge in him!" As we grow from the nourishment of that relationship, we become real with our time with God, and, because of that time spent with God, we become real and honest in our relationships with others.

I Peter 2:3 tells us, "For you have tasted the kindness of the Lord." When we spiritually taste the attributes God has shown toward us, forgiveness, love, understanding, and acceptance, we demonstrate those traits we have received to others. Let us be real this week as we show others in our conduct what God has shown us.

Blessings to all,
Chaplain Krupnik

My Musings

Light-
_____
_____
_____
_____
_____
_____
_____

Life-
_____
_____
_____
_____
_____
_____
_____

Lead-
_____
_____
_____
_____
_____
_____
_____

The Reason for the Season

As we are now in the midst of the Christmas season, my schedule is full of Christmas parties and events. I always enjoy the Christmas decorations, which we usually put right after Thanksgiving so that we can enjoy them a long time. There is also all of the Christmas shopping to find everyone the "perfect" gift. My wife even had enough courage to go out the day after Thanksgiving this year. However, in all of the excitement and activities, it is easy to lose sight of the real meaning of Christmas. We celebrate Christmas because it is the celebration of Christ's birth, the best gift of all. God sent His Son as a gift to us, that through His Son's death and resurrection, we could receive the gift of God's grace and salvation. Through the price paid by Christ, we are able to experience God's forgiveness. (Scripture reference), "God demonstrated His love for us in that while we were yet sinners, Christ died for us."

When we have experienced the forgiveness and grace of God, we, in turn, should show others that same forgiveness and grace. Our lives should be a reflection of God, and the peace and good will that comes from Him. The best Christmas gift that we can give to others this year is to show them the peace, forgiveness and grace that God has given to us through our thoughts, words, and actions. People will truly be blessed in our presence and feel the love of God if we allow that love to flow through us. What a great way to bless others and honor God this Christmas!

Blessings to all,
Chaplain Krupnik

My Musings

Light-

_____

_____

_____

_____

_____

Life-

_____

_____

_____

_____

_____

_____

Lead-

_____

_____

_____

_____

_____

_____

Doing Right

If you are a football junkie like I am, I hope you had your fill over the holiday season. Thank you to all spouses that tolerate the football junkies during this time of year.

Toleration in our relationships is so important. I believe that God is tolerant of each and every one of us. Toleration does not mean approval of behaviors that are harmful to ourselves or to others. Toleration is the acceptance of our behaviors that make us different and unique. God is tolerant of us because of the love He has for us.

I Peter 2:20-21 states, "For what merit is there in standing punishment for doing wrong? But if you bear patiently with suffering for when you are doing right, this is pleasing to God. To such experience you have been called; for Christ also suffered for you and left behind an example, that you might follow in His footsteps." God's love for us is so abundant and overwhelming that, not only is He tolerant of us, He actually suffered for us despite our faults and inconsideration of His love. Unless we make His love active in our lives by showing it to ourselves and each other, it is not worth a whole lot. For me, it is easier to be tolerant of others than to be tolerant of my own faults. God wants us to accept ourselves for who and what we are, because of His love for us. That acceptance of ourselves leads to improved toleration of others. Through that toleration of ourselves and others, our relationships become better and aspects of our lives become enriched. Let us strive to be tolerant of ourselves and others through God's love for us.

Blessings to all,
Chaplain Krupnik

My Musings

Light- _____

_____

_____

_____

_____

_____

Life- _____

_____

_____

_____

_____

_____

Lead- _____

_____

_____

_____

_____

_____

_____

Continuing the Dream

The base celebrated Martin Luther King, Jr.'s birthday with a prayer breakfast this past week. The event was well attended. Dr. Martin Luther King, Jr.'s life dream, for which he sacrificed his life, was to put an end to discrimination, segregation, and prejudice in our nation.

The Bible is clear on the equality of all people before God. In Acts, 10:34-35, we read, "Then Peter began to speak: I now realize how true it is that God does not show favoritism but accepts men from every nation who fear him and do what is right."

Prejudice is premature judgment; it is to form an opinion, usually unfavorable, before the examination of the facts. The erection of religious, political, economic and social barriers between one group and another makes it impossible for members of the two groups to fully know, appreciate, and understand each other.

We cannot build a good world if we disregard the moral and ethical laws established by God and revealed through the Scriptures. God's purposes include the whole person, and all persons. We can demonstrate our love for God by demonstrating our love for all persons in concrete ways.

When we are willing to "love our neighbor as ourselves," then we are beginning the process to end the prejudice in our lives. Let us begin that process and continue the vision that Martin Luther King, Jr. had for this nation and the vision that God has always had for His creation.

Blessings to all,
Chaplain Krupnik

My Musings

Light-

_____

_____

_____

_____

_____

_____

Life-

_____

_____

_____

_____

_____

_____

Lead-

_____

_____

_____

_____

_____

_____

_____

_____

The Wrong Kind of Networking

I was invited to watch the football games at someone's home this past weekend (what else, right!). While we were watching the games, on the network we were engaged in conversation during the commercials. One of spouses asked what we were discussing. I remarked that we were networking, otherwise known as gossiping.

The Bible is very direct about the type of networking that is wrong and harmful, and that is "backbiting". The modern translations uses the terms, "malice and deceit". I Peter 2:1-3 states, "Therefore, rid yourselves of all malice and all deceit, hypocrisy, envy and slander of very kind. Like newborn babies, crave pure spiritual milk, so that by it you may grow up in your salvation, now that you have tasted that the Lord is good."

The wrong of backbiting is a wrong about untruth and half-truths. Some rules of conduct that one should consider before saying anything about another are: (1) Is it the truth? (2) Is it fair to all concerned? (3) Will it build goodwill and better friendships? (4) Will it be beneficial to all concerned?

People who are backbiters have no respect or regard for others. They only think of themselves. The wrong of backbiting is the wrong of a coward. The wrong of backbiting involves talking about another when he or she is absent. It means criticizing people behind their backs. It means assigning motives to and interpreting the acts of people without any knowledge of the circumstances.

As I wrote this article I felt convicted about how I measure my conversations, and I hope you will too. The best thing we can do is to resist backbiting. Let us vow to resist backbiting and build up the community that we are in with encouraging words about one another.

Blessings to all,
Chaplain Krupnik

My Musings

Light-

_____

_____

_____

_____

_____

_____

Life-

_____

_____

_____

_____

_____

_____

Lead-

_____

_____

_____

_____

_____

_____

_____

An Introduction to Winning

The championship game began with the introductions of some of the team members to a national audience. The introductions were a public acknowledgment of some of the players that were responsible for the teams' ability to compete in the championship game. The championship game is a cumulative event of winning for an entire football season. Only one team goes home a winner.

The Bible addresses winning in a different way. Proverbs 11:30 tells us, "He who wins souls is wise." What does winning souls mean? I believe it means that all of us have an obligation out of our devotion to God to introduce or reintroduce others to God.

The first disciple to follow Jesus was Andrew. After meeting Jesus, he went and found his brother, Peter, and introduced him to Jesus. From that introduction, Christ used Peter in a dynamic way to build His church.

When we introduce someone to God, we are presenting a winning situation that will last for an eternity. All of us potentially are part of that winning team that belongs to God. We need to follow up on the introductions and participate in our championship game of life with a spiritual commitment to God and to each other.

The championship game of life has eternal consequences. Let us all help each other as teammates to celebrate and share in the victory that has already been won, and to go home a winner.

Blessings to all,
Chaplain Krupnik

My Musings

Light-
_____
_____
_____
_____
_____
_____

Life-
_____
_____
_____
_____
_____
_____

Lead-
_____
_____
_____
_____
_____
_____
_____

Pursuing the Spiritual Ring

This past Saturday I went to watch my son play in a basketball game in Arizona for the class 2A state championship. The team, the Valley Christian High School Trojans of Chandler, Arizona, won the game and was crowned state champion for class 2A. To be the state champions had been the goal for the entire season. The team had a motto among the players, "30-1 don't mean a thing without a ring."

The championship ring is the symbol of complete victory. All of us that have a relationship with God have a spiritual championship ring. After the victory, the team went to the half court circle at the America West Arena and sang the Doxology. The singing was to me an acknowledgment, not just of an emotional and physical victory, but of a spiritual victory as well. In Romans 8:37-39 we read, "No, in all these things we are more than conquerors through him who loved us. For I am convinced that neither death nor life, neither angels nor demons, neither the present nor the future, nor any powers, neither height nor depth, nor anything else in all creation, will be able to separate us from the love of God that is in Christ Jesus our Lord." The verses are an acknowledgment that we are more that just conquerors (champions) with God. We are his creation and, as such, our lives should be lived as champions with the victory already won.

As champions, we should be leaders and examples for others to follow. When we feel defeated emotionally, physically, and spiritually, the spiritual ring of victory that God has given us is a reminder of the encouragement and strength that we find in his Spirit every day. As we walk with God daily, our lives should exemplify the victory that has been won for us, and from which nothing can separate us. Let us walk daily with God as champions.

Blessings to all,
Chaplain Krupnik

My Musings

Light-

_____

_____

_____

_____

_____

_____

Life-

_____

_____

_____

_____

_____

Lead-

_____

_____

_____

_____

_____

_____

The Unity of the Spirit

On Sunday, we had a baptism of one of our adult members at the chapel. The baptism was a public testimony of the members' commitment in faith to God. It was also an event that brought unity of spirit to the congregation. On Thursday, March 7, 2002, the Battle Color Ceremony will take place at MCLB Barstow. It is an event that brings a spirit of unity between the base and the community.

Why is it so important to have a spirit of unity? Because in unity we are more successful as a community and as individuals than we are alone and isolated. The Bible addresses the need for us to maintain unity in spirit. While in prison, Paul the Apostle wrote in Ephesians 4:1-3, "As a prisoner for the Lord, then, I urge you to live a life worthy of the calling you have received. Be completely humble and gentle; be patient, bearing with one another in love. Make every effort to keep the unity of the Spirit through the bond of peace." If we are to promote a spirit of unity, human pride that is harmful must go. Instead, we should encourage one another with honor. We are to have a modest view of self rather than an exaggerated sense of our importance. Many conflicts within our lives come as a result of someone desiring more credit than the person has received. To have unity in spirit, we are to be gentle. This means to be gentle and sensitive and responsive to the needs of others. We are to practice patience with respect to things over which we have no control. To have unity of spirit also requires us to practice patience with respect to people. We need to bear up under the burdens of life and not lose courage. The final trait that we need to exhibit is love. This kind of love toward people is a persistent, unbreakable spirit of good will not dependent on the loveliness of the recipients.

Let us build together the Unity of the Spirit in the community, in our homes, and in all of our relationships.

Blessings to all,
Chaplain Krupnik

My Musings

Light-
_____
_____
_____
_____
_____
_____

Life-
_____
_____
_____
_____
_____
_____

Lead-
_____
_____
_____
_____
_____
_____
_____

Faith, Community, Accountability

Driving down the interstate, I noticed a semi-trailer that had printed on the rear of the trailer, "Faith, Community, Accountability." I want to focus on the last word of the three "accountability." To have accountability, one is responsible and answerable for one's actions. The accountability that we should have in our personal lives is not only for things that are seen, but unseen things as well. Psalm 44:21 states, "Would not God have discovered it, since He knows the secrets of the heart?" If we were required to answer to someone for all of our actions, seen and unseen, would it or would it not make us a better person, spouse, parent, employee, employer, and citizen?

We often hold others accountable to a higher standard than we personally practice. If we practiced accountability daily in our lives, what a positive impact that would have on all of our relationships.

The idea of accountability includes discipline. Discipline has a positive and essential place in our lives. Deuteronomy 8:5 states, "Know then in your heart that as a man disciplines his son, so the Lord your God disciplines you." Discipline helps us to grow and to be more accountable for the consequences of our actions.

Hebrews 12:11 states, "No discipline seems pleasant at the time, but painful. Later on, however, it produces a harvest of righteousness and peace for those who have been trained by it." The harvest of righteousness is the consequence of our accountability. There is a peace and contentment that accompanies accountability, knowing in our heart and mind that we have done the right thing. Let us help each other be accountable for our actions in all that we do.

Blessings to all,
Chaplain Krupnik

My Musings

Light- _____

_____

_____

_____

_____

_____

Life- _____

_____

_____

_____

_____

_____

Lead- _____

_____

_____

_____

_____

_____

Open Space

In any direction that you drive from our Barstow community, you see a lot of open space. That open space can mean different things to different people. For some, it might mean freedom; for others, imprisonment. Living in our community can be great or difficult. How can we have such extremes when living in the same community? I believe that part of it is an understanding of the purpose and reason of why we are here. Another reason is how much we are involved in the community. Do we take advantage of what the community offers? Can our community do more? Part of the success in any community is the communication that takes place among its members.

From my perspective, communication has a spiritual aspect. In the book of Romans, Paul the Apostle gives some guidelines about our involvement with the body (community of members). Romans 12:3 tells us "not to think more highly than he ought to think"; in other words, not to be conceited. Romans 12:5 states, "We, being many are one body." We are all part of the community in which we live. Romans 12:9 advises us to "abhor that which is evil; cleave to that which is good." Within our community, we need to stand for what is good and resist the evil that is around us. Romans 12:12 instructs us to be "patient in tribulation." Constant complaining and seeking sympathy about the circumstances in which we find ourselves isolate us from our relationships within our community.

When we focus on God and we see the open space within our community, we find a place where we fit in and enjoy the freedom of being in our great Barstow community. Let us apply the principles of Paul and make the effort to be a part of our community.

Blessings to all,
Chaplain Krupnik

My Musings

Light-

_____

_____

_____

_____

_____

_____

Life-

_____

_____

_____

_____

_____

_____

Lead-

_____

_____

_____

_____

_____

_____

_____

Driving Forward

Of the more thought provoking commercials on television today, and I am not referring to the one with the hampster, is the one where the gentleman is driving backwards in his car to reduce the mileage accumulation. Of course, what he is doing is foolishness.

The Bible would say that the man is building a house upon sand. The Sermon on the Mount closes with the parable of the wise and foolish builders. Matthew 7:24-27 states, "Therefore, whosoever heareth these sayings of mine, and doeth them, I will liken him unto a wise man, which built his house upon a rock; And the rain descended and and the floods came, and the winds blew and beat upon that house; and it fell not, for it was founded upon a rock. And everyone that heareth these sayings of mine, and doeth them not, shall be likened unto a foolish man, which built his house upon the sand. And the rain descended, and the floods came, and the winds blew and beat upon that house; and it fell and great was the fall of it."

The Sermon on the Mount contains spiritual teachings that Jesus taught to give us a greater understanding about our relationship with God. As was then and is now, the teachings of Jesus are forward thinking. I encourage all to read the Sermon on the Mount and put our cars in gear to drive forward and not backward as we apply the wisdom that God has given us to our every day lives.

Blessings to all,
Chaplain Krupnik

My Musings

Light-

_____

_____

_____

_____

_____

_____

_____

Life-

_____

_____

_____

_____

_____

_____

_____

Lead-

_____

_____

_____

_____

_____

_____

_____

Carve the Blessings

We celebrate this weekend religious observances of our various faiths. The observances focus on the blessings, restorations, assurances, and forgiveness that God has given. It is a remembrance of what God has done with his people. This week I want to pass on to you an article that I have received via the e-mail from a close friend. It is reminder to me that the permanent blessings God has given us through our relationships with him and others need to be carved in stone and our spiritual, emotional and physical hurts we have received from others written in sand. There is a story that tells of two friends who were walking through a desert. During some point in the journey, they had an argument and one friend slapped the other one in the face. The one who got slapped was hurt, but without saying anything, he wrote in the sand:

"TODAY MY BEST FRIEND SLAPPED ME IN THE FACE".

They kept walking until they found an oasis where they decided to take a bath. The one who had been slapped got stuck in the mire and started drowning, but his friend saved him. After he recovered from the near drowning, he wrote on a stone:

"TODAY MY BEST FRIEND SAVED MY LIFE ".

The friend who had slapped and saved his best friend asked him, "After I hurt you, you wrote in the sand and now you write on a stone, why?"

He replied, "When someone hurts us, we should write it down in sand where the winds of forgiveness can erase it away, but when someone does something good for us, we must engrave it in stone, where no wind can ever erase it.

LEARN TO WRITE YOUR HURTS IN THE SAND AND TO CARVE YOUR BLESSINGS IN STONE!

Blessings to all,
Chaplain Krupnik

My Musings

Light-
_____
_____
_____
_____
_____
_____

Life-
_____
_____
_____
_____
_____
_____

Lead-
_____
_____
_____
_____
_____
_____
_____

Carrying out the Intent

The last couple of weeks Marine Corps Logistics Base has been visited by military and civilian dignitaries. These visits are an acknowledgment of the great value the base and the Barstow community has in our national defense. One of our visitors addressed the officers about his desire to have his intent and purpose as a leader carried out at all levels in his command, both military and civilian.

We also have just completed religious holidays that have given God's intent and purpose for us spiritually. Are we as individuals and as a community carrying out God's intent and purpose? The religious holidays that we have just celebrated express God's desire for us to be free from bondage, both physically and spiritually. The intent from God is for us to take that message and make it a part of all that we do in our lives. Our response can be found in a parable that Jesus told. In Matthew 21:28-31 we read, "What do you think? There was a man who had two sons. He went to the first and said, 'Son, go and work today in the vineyard.' 'I will not,' he answered, but later he changed his mind and went. Then the father went to the other son and said the same thing. He answered, 'I will, sir,' but he did not go. Which of the two did what his father wanted? 'The first,' they answered." The first son appeared to be disrespectful but actually went and carried out the intent and purpose of the father and, by his actions of service, was actually respectful of his father's command. The second son, although appearing to be respectful, was disrespectful of his father's command by not carrying out the intent and purpose of his father.

We make daily choices about carrying out God's intent and purpose. If you are like me, many times I will say "no", but after the Spirit of God helps me think about it, I say "yes" by my actions. Let us do our best this week by saying "yes" to God as His Spirit leads us.

Blessings to all,
Chaplain Krupnik

My Musings

Light- _____

_____

_____

_____

_____

_____

Life- _____

_____

_____

_____

_____

_____

Lead- _____

_____

_____

_____

_____

_____

_____

Dealing with Disappointment

The traffic going back and forth on the weekends from Las Vegas and Los Angeles is interesting to observe. I have often wondered how many have been disappointed by the weekend events. They sure drive like they are disappointed and mad about something. In James 4:13-15 we read, "Now listen, you who say, 'Today or tomorrow we will go to this or that city, spend a year there, carry on business and make money.' Why, you do not even know what will happen tomorrow. What is your life? You are a mist that appears for a little while and then vanishes. Instead, you ought to say, 'If it is the Lord's will, we will live and do this or that.'"

It is good to have goals, but goals will disappoint us if we leave God out of them. There is no point in making plans as though God does not exist, because the future is in His hands. What would you like to be doing ten years from now? One year from now? Tomorrow? How will you react if God steps in and rearranges your plans? Plan ahead, but hold your plans loosely. Put God's desires at the center of your planning; He will never disappoint you. Life is short no matter how many years we live. We should not think that we have a lot of time remaining. Every day we have should be a day we live for God. When we live for God, all that we do takes on a different meaning and purpose. The time we have is prioritized to that standard and guess what? We have less and less disappointment because we are spending our time on things that are important. When disappointment does come, our faith is already in place to see us through because we know we are not alone; we are walking with God.

Blessings to all,
Chaplain Krupnik

My Musings

Light-

_____

_____

_____

_____

_____

Life-

_____

_____

_____

_____

_____

_____

Lead-

_____

_____

_____

_____

_____

_____

Into the Woods

On Friday, I attended a play/musical entitled, "Into the Woods". It is a grown up version of several childhood fairy tales like "Little Red Riding Hood", "Jack and the Beanstalk," Cinderella", etc. The theme of the play is essentially about how we enter "into the woods" of our lives (whether they represent the tough times, the conflicts, the growing experiences, or the temptations), and whether we come out of the woods having learned from the experience or having lost sight of our direction. The play focuses on the choices that we make and how those choices influence ourselves and those around us. The play goes on to show how we can make choices to get back on the right path.

The Hebrew scriptures in the wisdom literature of the Bible deal with two contrasting paths. The paths are rival ways that we can choose to follow: the path of the wicked or the path of the righteous. The people following the path of the wicked are those who forget God and keep Him at a distance. The people following the path of the righteous follow and live by the commands and instruction of the Lord.

All of us have, at times, gotten off the path of the righteous and followed the path of the wicked. It is a day-to-day struggle to stay on the path that brings honor to God and peace in our life amid the struggles that take place. In Proverbs 15:24 we read, "The path of life leads upward for the wise to keep him from going down to the grave(Sheol)." We find that path by following righteousness to wisdom and life. Let us encourage one another this week to follow the right path of righteousness as we go "Into the Woods" together.

Blessings to all,
Chaplain Krupnik

My Musings

Light-

_____

_____

_____

_____

_____

_____

Life-

_____

_____

_____

_____

_____

_____

Lead-

_____

_____

_____

_____

_____

_____

_____

Ninety-Nine and One

This week someone on the base was telling me about a new church that was being started in a different area of the country. The theme of the church being started was ninety-nine and one. The theme refers to the parable of the lost sheep found in Luke 15:3-7, "Then Jesus told them this parable: 'Suppose one of you has a hundred sheep and loses one of them. Does he not leave the ninety-nine in the open country and go after the lost sheep until he finds it? And when he finds it, he joyfully puts it on his shoulders and goes home. Then he calls his friends and neighbors together and says 'Rejoice with me; I have found my lost sheep.' I tell you that in the same way there will be more rejoicing in heaven over the sinner who repents than over ninety-nine righteous persons who do not need to repent.'"

There are times in our lives when we feel like the one lost sheep, when we have strayed far away from the security of the Shepherd and His flock. We feel like no cares about us, not even God. But Jesus is telling us today that this is not the case. God does care about us and He looks for those especially that have wandered away. But we have to want to be found. We have to respond when the Shepherd calls. We have to allow ourselves to be picked up by the Shepherd and carried back to the flock. We respond to the call and carrying from God by asking for forgiveness, turning away, and not looking back on the sin that has been committed. That is when the rejoicing takes place, when we allow God to carry us back to where we need to be.

If you are feeling lost today and you feel no one cares, God does and He is calling to you right now. Please respond to His call. We need not ever be lost again in God's hands.

Blessings to all,
Chaplain Krupnik

My Musings

Light-

_____

_____

_____

_____

_____

_____

Life-

_____

_____

_____

_____

_____

_____

Lead-

_____

_____

_____

_____

_____

_____

_____

Fan or Follower

I attended the Mayor's Prayer Breakfast last week. It was well attended and the keynote speaker provided an inspirational message. One of the points made by the speaker was whether we are a fan or a follower in what we believe. The dictionary defines a fan as "an enthusiastic devotee." A follower is someone who "follows another in regards to his ideas or beliefs." It is also defined as someone who "imitates" or "copies." The difference is the practical application. Are we a fan of our faith? Are we a follower of our faith?

There is nothing wrong in being enthusiastic for what we believe in. But the enthusiasm has to be applied in our everyday actions. If our everyday actions do not reflect our enthusiasm that we demonstrate during our times of worship, then we are just a fan. If our actions do reflect our enthusiasm, then we are a follower. Psalm 1 tells us, "Blessed is the man who does not walk in the counsel of the wicked or stand in the way of sinners or sit in the seat of mockers. But his delight is in the law of the Lord, and on his law he meditates day and night. He is like a tree planted by the streams of water, which yields its fruit in season and whose leaf does not wither. Whatever he does prospers. Not so the wicked. They are like chaff that the wind blows away. Therefore the wicked will not stand in the judgment nor sinners in the assembly of the righteous. For the Lord watches over the way of the righteous, but the way of the wicked will perish." As we delight in the law of the Lord and obey the teachings that God has given us, let us do so with enthusiasm as we make a practical application in our everyday actions as a follower of what we believe in.

Blessings to all,
Chaplain Krupnik

My Musings

Light-
_____
_____
_____
_____
_____
_____

Life-
_____
_____
_____
_____
_____
_____

Lead-
_____
_____
_____
_____
_____
_____
_____

Marketing MOM

The last couple of weeks the advertisers have been marketing MOM everywhere. They are good reminders for all of us to do something nice for the moms in our lives at least once a year, if not more. The marketing of MOM gives us that push and reminder that maybe we are taking for granted the moms around us and all the hard work that they do.

The Bible markets the qualities that moms are to have. In Proverbs, chapter 31, a list of those qualities is provided. Those qualities are praiseworthy as we read in verses 28-31, "Her children arise and call her blessed; her husband also, and he praises her: 'Many women do noble things, but you surpass them all.' Charm is deceptive, and beauty is fleeting; but a woman who fears the Lord is to be praised. Give her the reward she has earned, and let her works bring her praise at the city gate."

Thomas Edison said of his mother, "I did not have my mother long, but she cast over me an influence which has lasted all my life. The good effects of her early training I can never lose. If it had not been for her appreciation and her faith in me at a critical time in my experience, I should never likely have become an inventor. But her firmness, her sweetness, her goodness were potent powers to keep me on the right path. My mother was the making of me." The moms that we have may not have all the ideal qualities of the Bible or of Thomas Edison's mom. But the moms we have belong to us. They are our moms. Let us praise them the best way that we can this weekend for all the beneficial influence they have given us.

Blessings to all,
Chaplain Krupnik

My Musings

Light-

_____

_____

_____

_____

_____

Life-

_____

_____

_____

_____

_____

Lead-

_____

_____

_____

_____

_____

_____

With Great Power Comes Great Responsibility

This week I saw the latest super hero movie. One quote from the movie, "With great power comes great responsibility" was worth remembering. The super hero in the movie had to balance decisions based on the power that had been obtained and the responsibilities that surrounded the character.

God's grace is one of the most divine subjects of spiritual power that is given to all of us of faith. Grace is intended to empower us with the knowledge that we are forgiven. That empowerment of forgiveness should give us a desire to serve God. Our desire to serve is based on the responsibilities that we have been given through our calling, whatever that may be. With that purpose of service, we have a desire to do good works for God and for others. We receive direction and fulfillment for our lives because of those good works. The grace that transforms is seen in our actions. The Psalmist tells us that we learn these things from God. "Teach me to do thy will; for thou art God; thy spirit is good; lead me into the land of uprightness." (Psalm 143:10). God's will applies to everyone and to all things. We follow God's will by taking the responsibilities that we have been given and fulfilling them to the best of our ability with God's help. The important lesson for us is that we can obtain the strength that we need to render the service that God requires of us. God's grace enables us to do His will.

Blessings to all,
Chaplain Krupnik

My Musings

Light-

_____

_____

_____

_____

_____

_____

_____

Life-

_____

_____

_____

_____

_____

_____

Lead-

_____

_____

_____

_____

_____

_____

_____

Handling Criticism

Have you ever been made fun of or criticized for doing the right thing? The Hebrew scriptures provide for us a story of doing the right thing and being criticized and made fun of for it. The story is found in the Book of Nehemiah. If you have gone through a time of opposition, Nehemiah offers some counsel in dealing with critics. Please read the book of Nehemiah. The destructive critics make their attacks personal. They question your motives. They spread rumors. They run with other critics. They resist change. They are sarcastic. They use intimidation. They try to discourage those around you.

How does one deal with destructive critics or criticisms? The prophet Nehemiah used prayer. When criticized, ask God if the criticism is just. Pray for courage to change. Pray for those who are doing the criticizing. Pray for humility and the ability not to take things personal. Pray for wisdom, strength, and discernment to keep doing what is right. The prophet knew that the critics' problems were not with him, but with God. When you remind yourself God is in control, you recognize criticism for what it is and you do not allow it to dissuade you. God was persistent in doing the right thing. The best way at times to deal with critics is to outlast them, doing what you know God has called you to do.

Many times the races that we have in life do not go to the swift, but to the one who perseveres. If you are going through a time when it seems that everything you try is being met with opposition, if you feel like your critics are being destructive instead of constructive, recognize that when you step out on faith, follow God, and try to make a difference. You will be criticized. Expect it and deal with it through prayer, keeping the proper perspective, and being persistent.

Blessings to all,
Chaplain Krupnik

My Musings

Light-

_____

_____

_____

_____

_____

Life-

_____

_____

_____

_____

_____

Lead-

_____

_____

_____

_____

_____

_____

Fine Fathers

This coming Sunday will be Father's Day. The book of Proverbs gives us wisdom on the qualities of a fine man. The verses that I am addressing are found in Proverbs 20:3-7. Please read them.

A good dad must be a patient man. A good dad cultivates a pleasant, patient, positive surrounding. All of us growl every once and a while. But is it all the time? Make up your mind to be patient, and learn to make a strategic exit whenever you find yourself getting to the point of your growling turning into actions that are hurtful. Ask God for help and learn to smile more at your children. A good dad is a hard worker, doing the best that he can in the circumstances that he is in. He is diligent whose schedule includes time for his wife and children. A good dad is also a good listener. Good conversations cannot be turned on or off at will; you have to let them bubble up. The best conversations with children (especially teenagers) happen in relaxed settings, giving informal opportunities to open up. A good dad is a faithful friend; friends spend time with each other meeting the emotional needs, being a companion, confiding ones thoughts and feelings. A good dad shows that he is faithful to God in all that he does.

A good dad is a righteous man. He tries to do the right thing. He is committed to his faith, prayer and his place of worship. He is honest, modeling integrity for his children. The promise at the end of verse seven says that the children of such a man will be blessed. Happy is the child whose dad is a patient man, a hard worker, a good listener, a faithful friend, and a righteous man. Happy are the children of the dad whose God is the Lord. Let us work to have a Happy Father's Day every day in our homes.

Blessings to all,
Chaplain Krupnik

My Musings

Light-

_____

_____

_____

_____

_____

_____

Life-

_____

_____

_____

_____

_____

_____

Lead-

_____

_____

_____

_____

_____

_____

_____

Criteria for Contentment

I believe we all want to improve the quality of life that we have. One thing we can do along the way is to be content. Someone once told me, "It is not what we have, but what we enjoy that makes for a rich life, and the wise person understands that contentment is not having everything you want, but enjoying everything we have." Contentment is an elusive commodity in our society, yet contentment is one of the distinguishing marks of a person of faith. If you are practicing your faith, do you display contentment with those around you? The verses in the book of Philippians 4:11-13 tell us the following: "Not that I speak in regard to need, for I have learned in whatever state I am, to be content: I know how to be abased, and I know how to abound. Everywhere and in all things I have learned both to be full and to be hungry, both to abound and to suffer need. I can do all things through Christ who strengthens me."

What determines contentment? Does it depend on circumstances, church, or country? Dissatisfaction, discouragement and division are often symptoms of discontentment in our souls. Contentment must be equated with confidence in God over all His creation. Personal contentment in one's soul results in proper perspectives, priorities, and progress. Godliness and righteousness bring contentment into our lives. Pursuing them gives us an improved quality life that satisfies. Let us pursue the goal of improving our quality of life and be content along the way.

Blessings to all,
Chaplain Krupnik

My Musings

Light-
_____
_____
_____
_____
_____
_____

Life-
_____
_____
_____
_____
_____

Lead-
_____
_____
_____
_____
_____
_____
_____

Highway of Holiness

I have been away for a while from the Barstow community. I am glad to be back. One of things that I noticed upon my return was all of the construction projects in the area on the highways. Just a reminder to drive safely in those projects and slow down because the speed limit is enforced.

In the book of Isaiah, a highway is referred to as a "Way of Holiness." Isaiah 35:8-10 states "And a highway will be there; it will be called the Way of Holiness. The unclean will not journey on it; it will be for those who walk in that Way; wicked fools will not go about on it. No lion will be there, nor will any ferocious beast get up on it; they will not be found there. But only the redeemed will walk there, and the ransomed of the Lord will return. They will enter Zion with singing; everlasting joy will crown their heads. Gladness and joy will overtake them, and sorrow and sighing will flee away." For all of us to travel on the Highway of Holiness, we are required to have a faith commitment in our lives. That faith commitment reminds us of what God has done for us to bring salvation in our lives. Our response to that salvation that has been freely given to all is for us to live a life that is reflective of God's love. One of the ways God's love is displayed is by our holiness (doing what is right that brings honor to God).

The salvation that we have is not merely a past experience. It is a present reality. That reality requires dedication, the dedication to consistently journey with God on that highway. The highway we have may have potholes, construction, accidents and traffic on it. But if we stay focused on God as we travel, we can and will overcome all these things and have the joy that is waiting for us at the end of this highway. We will be entering into Zion one day as our final destination with that everlasting joy.

Blessings to all,
Chaplain Krupnik

My Musings

Light-

_____
_____
_____
_____
_____
_____
_____

Life-

_____
_____
_____
_____
_____
_____
_____

Lead-

_____
_____
_____
_____
_____
_____
_____
_____

Holy Reunions

I was attending an educational seminar this past weekend at a hotel. The hotel had many other events going on at the same time. It was interesting to see that three different high school reunions were taking place. Reunions can be very special times in which joys and successes can be shared. They can also be places where sorrows and failures are shared. Reunions are reminders that life, with its ups and downs, continues.

All of us have events in our lives that change and shape us. The Bible tells us to not be afraid of change because our faith is there to help us and sustain us through that change. Hebrews 13:5-6 states, "Let your conversation be without covetousness; and be content with such things as ye have; for he hath said, I will never leave thee, nor forsake thee. So that we may boldly say, The Lord is my helper, and I will not fear what man shall do unto me."

What sees us through times of change is our relationship with God. As with all relationships, the meaning and the value of it depends on how much time we spend with it and how much of ourselves we are willing to give to the relationship. Although God is always there for us, as He has promised to be, the strength that we can draw from our faith and that relationship depends on how strong our relationship is with Him.

We need to have constant "reunions" with God. Those reunions should be a time of celebration of our individual anniversaries with God, a reminiscence of what He has done for us in the past, a time when we tell God about our lives, our successes and failures, a time of recognition that God values us just the way that we are, and a time of fellowship to know that our relationship with God will continue. Let us continue to have our individual reunions with God daily, and allow that relationship with God to give us the strength that we need to help us through the changes in our lives.

Blessings to all,
Chaplain Krupnik

My Musings

Light-
_____
_____
_____
_____
_____
_____

Life-
_____
_____
_____
_____
_____
_____

Lead-
_____
_____
_____
_____
_____
_____
_____
_____

Overcoming Events

I watch, listen, and read about events that take place in our world. I am at times overwhelmed with all of the information that is available. Sometimes it makes me fearful to even go outside. The 9/11 commemoration will be taking place this coming week and we, as a nation, will be reliving those events that took place a year ago.

The events from 9/11 have changed many of our lives. The biggest change that I have seen is an awareness in our lives about what is important. The Scriptures reassure us about what is important, and that is our relationship with God. Isaiah 43.1-4 tells us, "Fear not, for I have redeemed you; I have called you by your name; You are Mine. When you pass through the waters, I will be with you; And through the rivers, they shall not overflow you. . . . For I am the Lord your God, the Holy One of Israel, your Savior. . . . Since you were precious in My sight, You have been honored, and I have loved you."

There are many things that we cannot control in our lives. However, as we live through events that take place in our lives, and as we look to the future, we are not to fear. God has promised that we are precious to Him, and that He will be with us through whatever we may face. His reassurance gives us the confidence that we need to overcome obstacles that fall in our path and to live the way God wants us to live. God wants us to devote our hearts and our lives to Him in all that we do. It is through that devotion that we understand God's commitment to us. Let us be committed to each other in the same way that God is committed to us. As we live with that commitment, we can help each other through the events that take place in our lives.

Blessings to all,
Chaplain Krupnik

My Musings

Light-

_____

_____

_____

_____

_____

_____

Life-

_____

_____

_____

_____

_____

_____

Lead-

_____

_____

_____

_____

_____

_____

_____

Hope for Healing

This week the reliving of the 9/11 experience has been difficult for our nation. The mourning and the grieving process brings out the best and worst of who we are as individuals and collectively as Americans. It seems that this week we have seen the best of who we are, both collectively as Americans, and individually.

As the healing process continues over 9/11, we also have an opportunity for healing in other relationships, for ourselves and also for our society. The grieving and mourning has brought us together as a nation. As we reflect about our one nation under God, the Scriptures direct us to God for healing. II Chronicles 7:14 states, "When I shut up the heavens so that there is no rain, or command locusts to devour the land or send a plague among my people, if my people, who are called by my name, will humble themselves and pray, and seek my face, and turn from their wicked ways, then will I hear from heaven, and will forgive their sin and will heal their land. Now my eyes will be open and my ears attentive to the prayers offered in this place."

I believe God has heard our prayers. We need to continue to humble ourselves before God and acknowledge the relationship that we do have with Him. Through this experience, our strength will grow and healing will take place as we rely more and more upon God.

Blessings to all,
Chaplain Krupnik

My Musings

Light-
_____
_____
_____
_____
_____

Life-
_____
_____
_____
_____
_____

Lead-
_____
_____
_____
_____
_____
_____

Everything is going to be all right

My mom, no matter how bad the situation was or how terrible things appeared, would speak these words, "Everything is going to be all right." The events that we have seen and experienced this year have caused concern, fear, and anxiety about the future. We look for solutions, comfort, hope, and reassurance. The future for us may seem uncertain, but what is certain is our relationship with GOD. In the book of Isaiah, we read in chapter forty, verse one, the following, "Comfort, comfort my people says your God." The words of the prophet Isaiah speak to us today that God does comfort his people. The comfort from God gives us the confidence we need to go through the difficulties we face in life.

Spiritual comfort can only come after sin has been forgiven. We all have strayed from the relationship we have with God. The farther we have strayed, the more uncertain we are in our lives. The more uncertain we are makes even the small problems seem like big ones. Why? Because we do not have the right relationship with God. We lack the confidence and support we need to have and we try to do things all on our own without insight or help from God. "Everything is going to be all right" are words of comfort only if we believe them. We can believe if we know that God has forgiven us of our sin. The comfort of hope that we desire comes when we make that spiritual adjustment of reconciling ourselves to God. The spiritual adjustment we make is a practical adjustment. Genuine repentance always finds its way into practical application. The practical application is in who or what we put our complete trust. If our trust is in God, then spiritual words of comfort have meaning and purpose and we can share them with others, because the same words that comfort us can comfort others. Let us comfort each other with "Everything is going to be all right".

Blessings to all,
Chaplain Krupnik

My Musings

Light-

_____

_____

_____

_____

_____

_____

Life-

_____

_____

_____

_____

_____

_____

Lead-

_____

_____

_____

_____

_____

_____

_____

Honor, Courage and Commitment

This will be my last article. I will be going to my next assignment, the U.S.S. Constellation (America's flagship). I want to thank everyone on the base and in the community for allowing me to be a part of your lives. I have grown from the experience in many ways and I hope that you all have grown from the many articles that have been written. I want to share one last story with you. When I was seventeen, I dropped out of high school and I decided that I wanted to me a marine. I went down to the recruiting office and I passed all of the entry level tests. The recruiting application required a parent's signature because I was under age. The sergeant came to my house for my mom's signature. My dad had died the year prior and I was the only one left at home. When my mom saw the sergeant with me, she broke down in tears. The sergeant looked at me and said, "Son, the Marine Corps needs you but your mother needs you more." With that, he shook my hand and left. I have always remembered that sergeant and what he said.

The naval service has the core values of Honor, Courage and Commitment. I believe that this sergeant represented those core values to himself, to my mom, to me, to the Marine Corps, and to this nation. I want to ask all of you, what do you represent? What are your core values? The values that we have are demonstrated by what we do in our actions, not what we say. The Scriptures use the example of a tree and its fruit. In Matthew 7:16-20, we read, "By their fruit you will recognize them. Do people pick grapes from thorn bushes, or figs from thistles? Likewise every good tree bears good fruit, but a bad tree bears bad fruit. A good tree cannot bear bad fruit and a bad tree cannot bear good fruit. Every tree that does not bear good fruit is cut down and thrown into the fire. Thus, by their fruit you will recognize them." I hope that I have planted some seed that God has turned into some fruit. I have not been perfect, but I have tried to uphold the core values of the naval service and to bear spiritual fruit of the higher calling that I have of being a minister of the Gospel. When you examine your life, I hope you are trying to bear the fruit that God has called us all to bear that have faith in Him. Thank you, once again, MCLB and the Barstow community for allowing me to be a part of your lives.

BLESSINGS TO ALL,
Your Chaplain

My Musings

Light-

_____

_____

_____

_____

_____

Life-

_____

_____

_____

_____

_____

Lead-

_____

_____

_____

_____

_____

_____

a Book's Mind

For more information about the author or purchasing bulk or single copies of this book, please e-mail the author at **info@solebalm.com**.

CPSIA information can be obtained
at www.ICGtesting.com
Printed in the USA
FFOW05n1810200617